10 Little Rules
for a
Double-Butted Adventure

by
Teri M Brown

ISBN: 979-8-218-62229-9

Published by Little Rules Publishing

Other books in the 10 Little Rules Series

10 Little Rules for a Blissy Life
by Carol Pearson

10 Little Rules for Your Creative Soul
by Rita Long

10 Little Rules of Hank
by Wendy Price

10 Little Rules for Finding Your Truth
by Micki Beach

10 Little Rules for Mermaids
by Amy Hege Atwell

10 Little Rules for the Modern Southern Belle
by Beverly Ingle

10 Little Rules for Serving You
by Amy Hege Atwell

10 Little Rules for Sharing Your Story
by Frank Winters

10 Little Rules When Good Jobs Go Bad
by Kathleen Goggin

www.10littlerules.com

DEDICATION

This book is dedicated to everyone who believed in me when I couldn't believe in myself, who loved me when I felt unlovable, and who cheered me on when I started to once again find my voice.

FOREWORD

I first met Teri at an author event in Southport, NC. I was mesmerized as she spoke about her grand double-butted adventure and her fiction writing.

We stayed in touch over the next two years, when it became fairly obvious she had the makings of a great 10 Little Rules book ... something that celebrates her achievement and honors the healing process sparked by doing something way outside one's comfort zone.

I'm honored Teri's beautiful story has found a home with us. Riding a tandem bike across the United States may not be in my future, or yours. Still, Teri's wisdom, grit and humor offer a path to grow and heal through whatever comes next in our lives. Be amazing.

Carol Pearson
Founder & Publisher
Little Rules Publishing

CONTENTS

Teri M Brown

INTRODUCTION

Have you ever wanted to have an adventure but figured you were too old or too fat or just too – fill in the blank? That was me. At the age of 54, I was out of shape – though, to be fair, round is a shape – unsure of myself, tired and worn out, and assumed somehow the world had passed me by. I was also in the middle of a messy divorce after a 14-year emotionally abusive relationship that only cemented each of these ideas into a reality I couldn't shake.

Then, my son's friend started an epic journey by planning to hike the Appalachian Trail. Ian kept a blog about his preparations and, once he began walking, he told his readers about his days and his insights. His quest lit a spark in me. I wanted my own epic quest – something that would prove to my children, my friends, but mostly to me, that I wasn't finished, that my life wasn't over, that my failed marriage didn't define me. I wanted to prove to myself I was a capable woman with a whole lot more to give in this life.

Ian finished his adventure in September; I began mine the following February when someone waltzed into my life who changed everything about what I thought was my truth. This someone, who is now my husband, helped me regain my confidence and my zest for life by introducing me to tandem cycling.

Prior to meeting Bruce, I hadn't been on a bike since college and hadn't ridden for the sheer joy of riding since middle school. While we were courting, he told me one day, "I've always wanted to ride across the United States on a bicycle."

That statement, along with our first 12-mile jaunt together, was all it took to make me embrace this adventure. So it began.

In the midst of getting in shape, determining what type of equipment we needed, discovering the basics of good cycling, and waking up each morning determined to finish what we had started together, I learned so much more than I imagined possible. This journey across the United States taught me that I am enough. I also learned volumes about people, relationships, God, and living a full life. Riding day in and day out gave me time to think and reflect. Ultimately, this adventure helped me to heal and to reclaim my self-worth and my personal power.

10 Little Rules for a Double-Butted Adventure is not a travelog, though you will learn quite a bit about crossing the United States at an average of 10.4 miles per hour. It is not a guide about cycling; though by the time you finish reading it, you will have a better grasp of what it is like to turn those pedals for three months straight. It also is not a manual about any specific experience – what I learned applies in equal measure to athletic endeavors, heading back to school, changing careers, completing some bucket list item, or any daunting life change.

This book at its core is an exploration of what I learned along the way – lessons that helped me regain a sense of purpose I will draw on until I take my final breath at some point in the future. I'm sharing it now with you, in hopes my story might touch you, inspire you, and support you as you find and live your own truths.

So, sit back and enjoy the ride.

RULE 1
Open Your Mind

You may think you understand the title of this book. It's straight forward, right? Double-butted adventures perfectly describe how my husband and I completed something substantial while riding a two-seated bike ... and you'd be correct, at least partially. Let me explain.

In our relationship, I am the creative one. Feel free to reread this sentence with the word emotional – it works just as well. I laugh. I cry. I experience vivid colors that take my breath away. I choose the perfect angle to take the perfect photo. When something goes wrong, my immediate response is to fall to pieces and suffer the agony of the situation before I have the ability to find a solution. On the other hand, when the situation is flawless, I dive in like a child with pigtails streaming behind.

Bruce is a civil engineer who spent 25 years in the military and another 10 working with government contracts. He is methodical and orderly. He fixes things. He rarely gets rattled. He doesn't do effusive emotions and doesn't have any urgent need to stop and take a photo. He is always prepared and has umpteen plans in his back pocket because he has learned the original plan never survives first contact with the enemy. He's the other half of the name.

To build a tandem bike, a special technique is used to weld the tubes of steel together. The center of the tube is thinned out to remove some of the weight. However, at the ends where the welding takes place, the steel needs to be thicker. This method is called double butting. I had no idea this technique existed when I came up with the title of our adventure. Yet the dual meaning fits us beautifully. He is the yang to my yin.

I loved the title choice as a funny play on words. He agreed to the name as a technical way to explain a process. We are both correct – neither is wrong. We could let this divide us, each sure in our rightness. We could spend hours debating the 'real' reason behind the title, letting these debates pull us into different camps where we've dug in our heels, needing only to be right. Or we could marvel at our differences and enjoy how they come together with ease, creating an amazing togetherness that would not be possible alone. We've chosen the latter.

This idea that there is more than one way to see something – and just as importantly, more than one correct answer – is something sorely missing from today's society. As people, we have begun to focus on our differences and separate into groups, when it would be so much kinder to consider how our distinctions enrich the world.

Preparing for this adventure across the United States showed me again and again that there isn't just one solution. It takes time, patience, and a willingness to explore and experiment to find what works best for my unique situation.

For example, let's look at the saddle saga.

Bicycle saddles (I called them seats until Bruce, after several months of trying, trained me in the correct terminology) are not made for women. The nose of the saddle pushes in all the wrong places, and a poorly placed pothole can leave a woman feeling violated.

The back of the saddle must accommodate the rider's sit points – the point on each cheek that bears the majority of the weight when sitting. A woman's sit points depend on the width of her hips, the angle at which the legs meet the hip sockets, and how far forward she leans while riding, among other things. Likely, due to the ability to bear children, a woman's sit points are significantly different from a man's.

Bruce can place his fanny on just about any saddle, adjust himself a bit, and ride without issue. On a long tour, he will want to find the right saddle, but for an hour or two, he can deal with anything.

For me? If I don't have the perfect seat, within ten minutes I have a pain that begins to run from my groin to my knee. Unless I dismount, the throbbing becomes so intense that pedaling is excruciating.

In the year leading up to our adventure, I tried six seats before finding the one I believed I could use day in and day out – as long as I had padded shorts and lots of lube.

My first saddle felt like riding on a cement block. My second had great gel but the gel wasn't located in the same vicinity as my sit points. The third was wider and had great gel but felt like I was trying to pedal with a log between my legs. The fourth had a long drop nose, a relief port (hole down the center of the saddle), and gel, but the nerve pain happened with every ride. The fifth was an old seat of Bruce's that seemed to be perfect. Unfortunately, it was falling apart and would never make it over 3,000 miles. At 15-years-old, it was no longer manufactured. By the time we left on the trip, I had chosen the Liberator X.

Many women I met along the way suggested other saddles, often informing me they had tried the Liberator and how much better the one they had was. No doubt they were telling me their reality – but their truth wasn't mine.

John Godfrey Saxe wrote a poem written in 1873 that speaks to what I discovered about personal certainty. (Saxe,1873)

THE BLIND MEN AND THE ELEPHANT

It was six men of Indostan
To learning much inclined,
Who went to see the Elephant
(Though all of them were blind),
That each by observation
Might satisfy his mind.

The First approached the Elephant,
And happening to fall
Against his broad and sturdy side,
At once began to bawl:
"God bless me!—but the Elephant
Is very like a wall!"

The Second, feeling of the tusk,
Cried: "Ho!—what have we here
So very round and smooth and sharp?
To me 'tis mighty clear
This wonder of an Elephant
Is very like a spear!"

The Third approached the animal,
And happening to take
The squirming trunk within his hands,
Thus boldly up and spake:
"I see," quoth he, "the Elephant
Is very like a snake!"

The Fourth reached out his eager hand,
And felt about the knee.
"What most this wondrous beast is like
Is mighty plain," quoth he;
"'Tis clear enough the Elephant
Is very like a tree!"

The Fifth, who chanced to touch the ear,
Said: "E'en the blindest man
Can tell what this resembles most;
Deny the fact who can,
This marvel of an Elephant
Is very like a fan!"

The Sixth no sooner had begun
About the beast to grope,
Than, seizing on the swinging tail
That fell within his scope,
"I see," quoth he, "the Elephant
Is very like a rope!"

And so these men of Indostan
Disputed loud and long,
Each in his own opinion
Exceeding stiff and strong,
Though each was partly in the right,
And all were in the wrong!

So, oft in theologic wars
The disputants, I ween,
Rail on in utter ignorance
Of what each other mean,
And prate about an Elephant
Not one of them has seen!

Each man in the poem experienced the elephant from a different angle and came away with a different understanding. This poem is insightful and humorous because we know what an elephant looks like and understand the foolishness in assigning a narrative by experiencing only a knee or trunk or tail.

The truth is, we are all guilty of being partially blind as we experience our daily elephants. We reach out and touch the differences and make our assumptions about the whole. There is no shortage of differences, starting with the most obvious like race, religion, politics, socio-economic status, and sexual orientation. A quick perusal of social media platforms provides even more reasons to separate. Breastfeeding. Eating organic. Vaccinations. And the most controversial, pineapple on your pizza.

Sure, we could let these things divide us. We could spend our time and energy creating groups that oppose those who stand firmly in the opposite camp.

Or we can order a pizza — half with pineapple and half without.

your turn...

Open your mind

Take a few minutes now to think about any differences of opinions you have with people in your life – family, friends, co-workers, neighbors, even your "friends" on social media.

How much time and energy do you put into defending your own position (either out loud or to yourself)? How do you feel when you're doing that?

What if you spent some of that time trying to see things from another point of view? How do you think you might feel doing that? (It's not always fun to consult our own biases ... and new information can even feel threatening. On the other hand, empathy can be a powerful peace maker.)

Are you always looking for differences, or can you start to search for more common ground? What happens when you're faced with a topic on which you absolutely cannot budge? Can you find some common ground to stand on?

_____

_____

_____

_____

_____

_____

_____

_____

_____

_____

_____

_____

_____

_____

_____

_____

_____

RULE 2
Expect Setbacks

When we think of progress, most of us consider a straight, smooth line from Point A – our starting place – to Point B – our goal. Someone trying to lose 20 pounds will lose one pound, then two, then three, until they have achieved their target. Someone putting together a desk from IKEA will insert Part A into Part B using Fastener C until the desk is ready for use. Someone who decides to ride across the United States on a tandem bicycle will pick their equipment, go on training rides, and begin the adventure until they've made it to Washington DC.

Except that's not how life works.

The reality is a birthday party comes along, the dieter chooses to eat cake and ice cream, and the result is weight gain instead of weight loss. The reality is what you thought was Fastener C was really Fastener D, so you must reassemble the desk three times before getting it right. The reality is going on an epic journey is not as easy as finding the perfect saddle, riding 1,000 training miles, and arriving at the Marine Corps Memorial.

With every adventure in life, setbacks will occur. What you choose to do about them is what matters.

My first experience with this life lesson came before Bruce and I were married – when the quest was still in the embryonic stages with no starting date and a nebulous idea of what we wanted to accomplish. We were in Maine, having evacuated from a hurricane. Rather than run from the storm, we chose to go on vacation, calling our exodus an e-vac-ation. While in Maine, we began riding the tandem on hilly terrain, something that is not possible when you live on the coast of North Carolina.

I kept a blog of our double-butted preparations and proclaimed with bold naivety that we would complete the Acadia National Forest loop the following day. I was upbeat and absolutely certain this outing would be another notch in my belt toward the completion of our great adventure. The truth is something that still stings a bit, despite understanding everything that kept us from completing the goal.

My post started with these words:

"Without wi-fi, I could have just forgone posting the blog, and you would have never learned about the disastrous outcome of the loop ride. Nonetheless, I promised I would be honest."

My intention was to tell readers about the ups and downs of adventure prep. However, I didn't think I'd have to report any significant downs. In my mind, the training would be a series of little ups that eventually took us on our adventure – and the adventure would be a series of ups that eventually took us across the United States.

I did expect poor weather. I understood we would face some massive hills. Yet I always believed each would be a minor blip, something we would mention while standing triumphant at the end of the day.

I never expected to have to tell everyone we failed. Nor did I want to tell everyone the failure was, in large part, due to me.

That particular day was cold, causing me to shiver despite my warm cycling clothes. We chose to start just outside Acadia, parking our truck near Eagle Lake. We put our 65-pound bulldog in the trailer to simulate carrying our gear and headed toward the park's entrance.

The first hill was challenging – steeper and longer than any we had so far attempted on the tandem together. To complicate matters, our bicycle wouldn't drop into the lower gears. We stopped as we got to the main gate, having gone a little over a mile. Bruce was so winded he was hanging over the handlebar. My legs ached, and I couldn't begin to imagine how I would make it 27 more miles plus another mile back to the truck when we were through.

Bruce decided we had bitten off more than we could chew. I choked down my tears. He assured me this was not my fault, but I KNEW otherwise.

Bruce is an experienced cyclist. He had been riding competitively for more than 50 years. He had over 25,000 miles of tandem experience, including traversing over the mountains in Austria, Germany, and Ireland.

I did not have those qualifications. I was not in good shape. I didn't have the strength to pedal hard enough. I was too heavy. I was nothing but a nerd. I had failed him.

The mantra "I am a failure" ran through my head going back to the car. As I got into the truck with Bruce assuring me this was not my fault, I couldn't hold back the tears. I was so disappointed in myself as I visualized the whole adventure falling apart. Since this wasn't about Bruce's abilities, the shortcoming had to be my own.

Bruce is a wise man. He let me have my pity party, but then he did something that at first confused me, but ultimately, gave me the courage to keep on trying. He took us to the outskirts of Southwest Harbor and said, "We are going to ride."

The gears were still stiff and making chunky noises, but we rode up and down hills into town. Then we started back. I made it up a long and arduous hill and felt proud of myself. On the second hill, the chain snapped. A link had bent due to the gearing problem. The mechanic at the bicycle shop showed Bruce the issue, and once we got back to our home in North Carolina, we were able to make the appropriate changes.

Without a doubt, this particular ride was not a straight path toward our goal. We discovered several things that needed attention before we set out on our adventure. For example, our gear set-up would never allow us to pedal over the mountains in Oregon, Washington, Idaho, Montana, or Pennsylvania.

We also realized we were trying to run before we walked. Despite Bruce's ability on the tandem, I was still new to this kind of riding. He cannot carry me and the trailer alone. Tandem cycling is, by definition, a dual effort. We had to consider both of our abilities and make appropriate decisions based on these facts.

In the end, this 'disastrous' ride helped us move forward with confidence. Without a doubt, I contributed to the issues we had that day. But so did Bruce by making assumptions about what we could accomplish. So did our equipment, which worked well on flat, coastal terrain, but not so well in Maine.

I would love to say this was our one and only setback, but I would be lying. We hit setback after setback after setback.

Our path to completion resembled a massive knot rather than any sort of straight line. We experienced health issues including broken bones, equipment issues, anxiety issues, and even global pandemic issues.

We intended to leave the coast of Oregon in May 2020. When COVID-19 began to rage, we (like so many others) believed the pandemic would disappear long before our start date. By the middle of March, we concluded that our plans had been derailed. In fact, we were 100% certain our adventure was a no-go. Bruce went to the garage, unloaded the tandem, and 'wept' – *because Marines do not cry*. For about three weeks, we did not ride. We didn't even talk about the trip or lack thereof. I tried to come up with alternatives, because seeing my husband despair over the adventure he had wanted to complete for the past 40 years was more than I could bear.

Our original plan had been to cycle in Germany during September the following year. If COVID died out, we could flip-flop our agenda and go to Germany first, then do our US cross-country adventure the following summer. It didn't take long to realize COVID wasn't going to be eradicated by September.

Then I suggested we try a winter ride, starting in January 2021. This would mean coming up with a new route that took us much further south, to accommodate riding conditions throughout the colder months.

We researched some that might make this possible, but they were not nearly as beautiful as the northern ride. Plus, the weather, though not as frigid as cycling up north, might be too cold to make the adventure enjoyable.

Then we spotted a trend. Some states and larger cities began to open up just a bit. The lockdowns weren't as tight. What if things opened up enough to allow us to take the trip despite COVID? We determined if we started the adventure by the middle of July, we could still finish before the cold weather set in. In the end, this is what we did. What appeared to be a huge blockade turned into a detour that, once again, didn't make our path straight and smooth.

When we arrived in Oregon, we found our progress forward was never as simple as we had anticipated.

Adventure plans made sitting at a kitchen table or a motel desk seem quite reasonable and achievable. Then ... real life happens. Muscles are sore. Winds don't do as they are told. That good night's rest wasn't as good as one would hope. Equipment doesn't work as promised. And myriad other things intervene to make advance planning just an outline to hang reality on.

This is why Bruce always quips, "Amateurs study tactics, professionals study logistics." Then he follows up with a history lesson.

During World War II, Patton was an amazing tactician. However, he drove his superiors crazy by over-running the supply line, putting his troops way ahead of needed supplies like food and gas. He was brilliant but never thought about the logistics of his plans. Doing so cost him men and equipment.

While I bemoaned the need to make yet another plan to accommodate some new issue, Bruce insisted we were still on our Plan A. Our original plan was to go across the US on a tandem bicycle. We were still following that plan despite the modified logistics. We changed dates, starting locations, ending locations, routes, and more – but in the end, we were still going to make our final goal; we were going to have our adventure.

As I reread my blog to prepare to write this book, I had to wonder why I insisted on writing about what would come tomorrow when three out of four times, the logistics changed – often in the middle of the night or while riding the next day. I was stuck with the idea that success lies along a straight line, despite overwhelming evidence this just simply is not true.

I will be the first to admit I did not handle all the change with grace. I cried on the side of the road more times than I can count. I griped. I grouched. I declared I was done. In the end, I did what I had to do and got on the bike and rode.

I came to see that marriage, in many ways, is like an adventure. It has its ups and downs, changes, and detours. And although my previous marriage hadn't lasted, didn't I find myself still along life's path? Hadn't I picked myself up, dusted myself off, and continued forward despite the pain?

The truth is that everything changes. Period. And that, my friends, is what I think the definition of "adventure" really means.

What about success? The key to success is not about the route but about how we choose to deal with the things that make us deviate from the straight line we imagined.

True success is handling these life adventures – this series of straight lines, squiggles, stumbling blocks, reversals, bumps, alternate paths, and even adjusted goals – until finally, you've made it to Point B.

your turn...

Expect setbacks

In any adventure, planning is crucial. Yet we all know plans go awry, for any number of reasons. Some people can shift gears without problem, while others struggle with the "hows," often letting them overshadow the "why."

How do you react to those sudden changes in the plan? Do they tend to throw you for a loop? Or do you take them in stride and shift accordingly? Or maybe somewhere in between?

Think back to a time when you experienced an unwanted and unexpected setback. How did you react at the time? Now think about what you learned – about yourself, about others, about life – while going through that challenge. Do you think you might handle a similar situation differently now?

How can you look at your life now as an adventure, rather than a straight path to the end?

Use the space on the next few pages to jot down your thoughts.

_____

_____

_____

_____

_____

_____

_____

_____

_____

_____

_____

_____

_____

_____

_____

_____

RULE 3
Do Hard Things

As humans, we are far more capable of accomplishing difficult tasks than we think we are. With gaping mouths, many people we met on our trip told us they could never ride across the United States on a bicycle – NEVER. The truth is, if they really wanted to, they could.

How do I know this? Because I did it – and if I can do it, anybody can.

I am not an athlete; I am a desk jockey. My career choice consists of sitting at a computer all day. I enjoy being active, but these activities include such things as walking along the beach at sunrise while picking up shells and chatting with others doing the same, kayaking in the calm waters of the Intercoastal Waterway on a lazy Sunday afternoon, or swimming laps in the community pool before devouring a delicious grilled meal. They do not include skydiving, running marathons, playing on sports teams, or becoming too sweaty for no apparent reason. Because of this, one might assume riding on a tandem bicycle across the United States would not be part of the plan.

Except I wanted an adventure, and I wanted *this particular* adventure. So, I set my mind to it, and I did it. But not without first learning how my mind has the ability to overcome what my body says it cannot do.

While dieting to prepare for this journey, I severely limited my calorie intake. The majority of my nutrition came from fat released into my bloodstream due to HCG shots. This made exercise difficult at best and, at times, impossible. The summer heat drained me, making cycling, swimming, and even walking a chore that required thought and preparation.

During this time, Bruce and I planned a trip to Oregon because I had never seen the Pacific Coast. Along with visiting relatives, we intended to do quite a bit of sightseeing. I was rewarded with an incredible sunset, sea lions, black sand, sea stacks, and mountains that rose right to the ocean's edge. It was on one of these 'moderate' mountain walks that I thought I might meet my Maker.

Our destination was the top of Spencer Butte. Google informed me a moderate trail hike to the crest would provide amazing views. I was game but concerned about Bruce. Not only is he disabled, but his arm was in a sling due to recent surgery. Although he can outride me any day of the week, walking is another matter, so I didn't want this little side trip to be too much for him.

I needn't have worried. He made it to the top with the skill of a mountain goat. I seriously considered what it would be like to die on the face of a mountain.

The moderate hike would have been challenging for me given my restricted calories. The difficult trail we took by mistake was ... beyond description. It was only a mile long, but there were times we were not hiking, but rock climbing, hunting and pecking for a decent foothold.

For reasons I still do not understand, I had not prepared myself well. With only a bottle of water and no snack, I had not considered my own issues, just Bruce's. By the time I realized I was in trouble, going back down would have been more dangerous than continuing.

With about 200 yards to go, I sat on a boulder with tears falling from my eyes. I had pushed myself as far as possible. Waving to Bruce to go ahead, I said, "Go on to the top. I'm done. I can't go further." Of course, he wouldn't leave me. He went forward but within sight and encouraged me to keep trying. My water was gone. I had no fuel left in my body and none to replace what I had spent. I couldn't move.

As I sat on the rock, contemplating this as my eventual burial site, I had something I will call a vision. Because of my religious views, I believe life here on this earth is a trial to help me grow and become more like my Father in Heaven. As hikers talked and laughed above me while enjoying the view, I understood in an instant how someone could come within reach to a glorious end but surrender before the battle was won. With just 200 yards to go, so near to my destination, I was not going to make it. The eternal perspective hit me. How sad that so many come so close, then give up.

I prayed for divine assistance, hauled myself up off the rock I had assumed would be my tombstone, spied another rock ten feet away and made that new rock my goal. Upon reaching the new rock, I half lowered, half fell onto it, cried some more, located a new goal ten feet away, and repeated and repeated. By ten foot increments, I crawled to the top.

Bruce said he was proud of me. My initial reaction was I had failed ... then I came to understand that I discovered something deep within me I didn't realize I had. I discovered that despite the real lack of energy and the real need to just quit, my mind had the ability to overpower my body and move me forward to my destination.

Although I still call this my Bataan Death March, this single experience propelled me through many demanding days on our adventure. I called on this inner mind strength a number of times when I couldn't go another foot ... including the day we headed to Glasgow, Montana.

The day was hot, getting to 97 degrees by midday. The mileage was long – we planned to ride 70 miles that day because there was no place to stay between our starting point in Malta and our destination in Glasgow. We had been told the roads were flat, but the truth was the entire 70 miles was one hill after another after another. The winds were blowing at 15 miles per hour ... in the wrong direction. We had to repair not one, not two, but three flat tires during our day's journey. And let's not forget the valley of mosquitoes that came at us in hordes and seemed to drink bug spray for breakfast.

At mile 56, we took a break at a rest area. We refilled all of our bottles, drenched all of our clothes with water, and I even took off my shoes and poured cold water over my feet trying to negate the effects of the heat. Even so, due to the low humidity and high winds, we were completely dry within minutes of leaving the rest area. When we hit our next hill, I was spent.

With about six miles to go, we stopped in front of an eight-foot high historic marker that cast a bit of meager shade onto the ground. Bruce put down a tarp, and I sat and cried.

"I can't go any further. I'm too hot. I'm too tired. I'm just done," I sobbed.

Bruce nodded along, knowing at this point in the trip I needed a good cry. He assured me that if he could call an Uber, he would, but we had no choice but to continue.

Just as I stopped crying, an errant cloud sprinkled a bit of rain and covered up the sun's piercing rays. Taking a deep breath, I said a quick prayer for the strength I would need, swung my leg over the bike and began to pedal. Moving forward was not easy. We wondered if we would make it. When we passed the "Welcome to Glasgow" sign, Bruce had to stop and recover. We rested one more time before coming to the first motel on the outskirts of town – that hole-in-the-wall became our oasis for the night because it had a shower, a bed, and a Flip-Burger right across the street. Our needs had been reduced to bare essentials.

Since finishing this adventure, I have realized I am capable of doing anything I set my mind to. The limits placed on me – by an abusive ex-partner or by myself – no longer exist.

Can I run a marathon? Yes, I am capable. Do I want to run a marathon? Not in this lifetime! But without a doubt, if that answer was yes, I am sure I would succeed.

your turn...

Do hard things

Think back to a time when you did something hard ... something you might have felt scared to face or knew would be a challenge. Where did you find the strength to begin? How did you feel when you accomplished it?

What are you facing now in your life that seems hard? Are you feeling any limits on what you can accomplish? Are those limits valid?

Imagine facing this hard thing with certainty that you can at least begin, and that you truly *want* to begin. What's the first step?

Who can you call on to find support for this new, hard, and worthwhile adventure?

Use the journaling space on the following pages to write your thoughts.

_____

_____

_____

_____

_____

_____

_____

_____

_____

_____

_____

_____

_____

_____

_____

_____

_____

_____

_____

_____

_____

_____

_____

_____

_____

_____

_____

_____

_____

_____

RULE 4
Enjoy the Downhills

This may seem obvious, but for me, it was not as intuitive as one might think. Sure, riding downhill is great. I had no need to pedal. The wind created a cooling effect as it rushed across my face. Racing down a hill gave me the sensation of flying – but only if I let it. In the beginning, I didn't allow that joy.

Each time we went downhill, all I thought about was the elevation we were losing. Why? Because I had worked so hard to gain that elevation, and I knew I would have to gain it all over again. Until we got out of the mountain ranges – hundreds of miles into our adventure – the destination was always "up."

Imagine, if you will, an hour of steady spinning up a hill at four miles per hour. To reach the top of the incline takes an hour of riding and two or three "butt breaks" – necessary breaks to take your fanny off the saddle. During this hour-long journey, the only time you stop pedaling is during these butt breaks. At times, the hill becomes steep, so you exert a bit more. Your breath comes out in puffs and the muscles in your thighs burn with the effort. Finally, you reach the goal. You arrive at the top. The downhill is long and smooth and lasts only minutes. Then, at the bottom of the down is another up – another hour of climbing.

Imagine how you'd feel seeing the downhill leading into another climb with no break in between.

These continuous cycles of up and down initially led to discouragement and a bit of anger. Why did I have to lose all I gained? Why was the road so hilly? Why couldn't I arrive at the top of the hill and have no more hills to climb? Such were my thoughts as we'd speed down the hill and then begin the next up – hill after hill for the first several days of our journey.

Until one day, Bruce said something that changed my way of thinking and created a huge paradigm shift. "The road is the road. Being upset that the road is going down and back up again doesn't change the facts."

I thought about that. A magical road fairy did not exist to smooth out the path or create a bridge from one hilltop to the next. The road was the road. The route we chose was the easiest course across the mountain ranges. We knew when we picked it we would be going over countless summits, and we knew, at least to some degree, that doing so would be difficult.

Then, I had the real epiphany. I wasn't enjoying the ups *or* the downs. I was spending so much time griping about the road not being flat, that even when the road was the best it could be – downhill – I wasn't enjoying the ride. I spent the first several days of our journey dreading every hill – both ways. What a waste!

If you've ever seen Thornton Wilder's drama *Our Town*, you'll remember one of the main characters, Emily, dies in childbirth but is given the chance to come back and relive her 12th birthday. Although she starts out this adventure with excitement, she soon realizes she had taken so much for granted when she was young, and says, "Do any human beings ever realize life while they live it – every, every minute?"

Most of my friends and acquaintances live for the future; when the babies are older, when the teenagers move from home, when they get that new job, when they finally retire, *then* they will be happy. Only when a certain set of circumstances are met – the end of a hill without another hill in sight – do they allow themselves to find joy.

While we wait for that time, that event, that one thing that will finally bring us everything our heart desires, we miss out on all the downhills. In fact, we even miss the glory of going up. Let me explain.

Bruce and I rode across the United States at an average of ten miles per hour. Our uphill pace was about half of that, and our downhill pace was three times faster. Although going down at 30 miles per hour was exhilarating, it was rarely awe-inspiring.

While flying down a hill nearing the speed of a car, I didn't allow myself to notice the wildflowers blooming or the eagle's nest built out of hundreds of thick sticks. I didn't take note of the difference in air temperature as we crossed over a creek bed heading to the river on the other side of the road. I didn't smell the dense, woody, earthy scent of the moss and ferns growing along the edge of the woods. I didn't hear the birds calling to one another or the buzzing of bees as they collected nectar. It wasn't until I learned to appreciate the downhills that I also learned to appreciate going up.

Enjoying the ride for the sake of the ride itself is not easy for me; I'm a real control-freak. I like things to be as planned – or as advertised. When a motel doesn't provide the amenities listed on their website, the route we are taking is not flat as touted on the GPS, the wind is not blowing from west to east as other cyclists stated would be the case, or the day was not sunny as the weather app predicted, I would get surly, railing against the motel or app or people who threw a wrench into my day.

Bruce, who is much better at accepting life as it is rather than as it 'should be,' would wait calmly for me to accept what was – occasionally suggesting the road is what the road is to remind me I'm not the one in ultimate control.

Reinhold Niebuhr wrote the famous poem called The Serenity Prayer. (Neibuhr, 1932). Most people can recite at least the beginning of the first stanza ...

> *God, give us grace to accept with serenity*
> *the things that cannot be changed,*
> *Courage to change the things*
> *which should be changed,*
> *and the Wisdom to distinguish*
> *the one from the other.*

I suspect most people, however, are unaware of the rest of the poem:

> *Living one day at a time,*
> *Enjoying one moment at a time,*
> *Accepting hardship as a pathway to peace,*
> *Taking, as Jesus did,*

This sinful world as it is,
Not as I would have it,
Trusting that You will make all things right,
If I surrender to Your will,
So that I may be reasonably happy in this life,
And supremely happy with You forever in the next.

Amen.

That first stanza, or even just the first line, makes a beautiful mantra for anyone, regardless of their faith or spiritual practice, to help them through their hard days.

Accept what cannot be changed – the course of the road. Courage to change what must be changed – injustice, anger, hatred. Wisdom to know the difference – the peace that comes when you aren't beating yourself against the rocks.

Yet it's the rest of the prayer that speaks to my core and aligns with the beliefs I hold dear. This prayer gives me hope. As I'm cycling slowly up the hills of my life and whizzing down when I reach a crest, I can know the ultimate control is with my Father in Heaven. If I enjoy the ride, both up and down, I can find a measure of happiness here. If I follow Him, I will be blessed with eternal joy. Anything in the middle that doesn't make sense or is unjust will be repaired by Him because this world and the people on it are His creation.

Did I ever discover true joy in the adventure? Sometimes, yes. There were days when I was able to let go and simply be. The adventure gave me a glimpse of what I'm aiming for. Getting to that goal, one of acceptance and joy in the here and now, is never a straight line ... and just like our adventure, that's okay.

your turn...

Enjoy the downhills

Think back to a time when you were able to "coast" a bit after accomplishing something hard. Did you take the time to truly enjoy it? If no, why not?

How about the uphill climb? Were you able to find a measure of joy in the hard work, so the downhill was that much sweeter? How do your beliefs, whether they align with mine or not, help you conquer your own uphill battles?

As you lean into your current uphill climb, can you envision yourself being grateful for the experience itself, knowing the payoff is coming?

Use the journaling space on the following pages to write your thoughts.

_____

_____

_____

_____

_____

_____

_____

_____

_____

_____

_____

_____

_____

_____

_____

_____

_____

_____

_____

_____

_____

_____

_____

_____

_____

_____

_____

_____

_____

_____

RULE 5
Focus On Now

One of my favorite things to do on our adventure was telling people we were riding across the United States on a tandem bicycle. As I started the sentence, the listener would smile and nod. They were expecting to hear something about us driving our car to an event or even being out for a day-long ride on a bike.

As I got to the words "across the United States," they would begin to focus a bit more on the words, maybe thinking "Ah, they are going on a long journey. I'll bet they are having fun." When I said a tandem bicycle, the reality of what we were undertaking dawned on them. The eyebrows would shoot up into hairlines, eyes would become wide, and mouths would form an upper-case O. Even behind a COVID mask, we could see jaws drop and hear the audible gasp. "You mean, on a bicycle? And you started in Oregon? Where are you riding to?"

Our answer was always the same, "To Washington DC...but not today."

"But not today" was always met with a laugh, but in truth that is how we made it across the United States. I quickly learned the day at hand was the only day to worry about.

Here's a post called "The Struggle Bus" as an illustration:

Have you ever had a day that, once started, you wished you could fast forward just to get to the end? That was today. For some reason, I had trouble from the first mile. My saddle didn't feel right. My legs felt crampy. My arms were tired. Had we been at home, I would have said, "Let's just go home and try again tomorrow."

Of course, we are not home, and going back wasn't an option. So, we pressed on and made it to Pomeroy - 42.6 miles.

Unfortunately, "Friday" wasn't feeling any better about itself than we were. We had big hills with grades at six percent or more. We had a quartering headwind for the last fifteen miles or so. We had temperatures into the eighties. We had arid, desert-like scenery where shade trees were rare.

About five or six miles from our destination, we stopped - in a rare shady spot. We didn't know how much further we had. We had been told there would be another steep uphill, so that was in the back of my mind. I was hot. So very hot.

I knew we didn't have more than ten miles, so I used some of my water to dump on my head, trying to create a cooling effect. The thought, "I just can't do this" was on repeat in my mind. I looked up at Bruce, who had too much concern in his eyes, and I started to cry.

I hate that about me. I wish I were stronger. But the tears came. And then, I put on my helmet, and we started out again.

Now, having eaten, showered, and lathered my nether regions with diaper rash cream, I'm feeling better. I can do this, but only one day at a time.

Our plan was to arrive in Cut Bank, and here we are! In fact, for the next several days, even weeks, we have few options. There are miles and miles between towns and there will be a headwind. But I will worry about tomorrow tomorrow and not before.

Riding across the United States on a bicycle is a huge undertaking. Although our destination was the Marine Corps monument in Washington, DC, we also had daily destinations, waypoints during the day, and sometimes, a goal of just making it to the next telephone pole before we would rest, yet again.

When people would ask us in complete amazement, "How is it possible to ride a tandem bike the entire way across the United States?" or "How will you climb over the Rockies?" Bruce would reply, "One pedal stroke at a time."

He was not being coy or trite; he was being honest. Our effort had to be on the day at hand, the hill in front of us at the moment, the current turn of the pedal. The harder the day, the more myopic the focus.

So many times, Bruce would say, "Okay, when we get to that next sign, we are going to stop." We would give it what we had left to give so we could make it to the sign where we would get off the bike, drink some water, eat a handful of granola, and add a bit more sunscreen or chamois cream for our nether regions before heading off once again.

One of the philosophies enjoying a renewed awareness is mindfulness. Oxford Languages defines this as a mental state achieved by focusing one's awareness on the present moment, while calmly acknowledging and accepting one's feelings, thoughts, and bodily sensations.

Although I never became good at the "calmly acknowledging and accepting" part, I became adept at focusing on the present moment – I had little choice.

Within days, we had created a routine:

- Awaken prior to the sunrise and fix breakfast.

- Break camp or load tandem after a motel stay.

- Fill the water bottles.

- Use the bathroom.

- Ride.

- Eat lunch.

- Ride.

- Arrive at the destination.

- Wash out clothes and hang them to dry.

- Set up camp.

- Shower.

- Bruce naps while Teri writes blog.

- Eat supper.

- Do logistics for the next day.

- Sleep.

- Repeat.

This means all day I focused on the day at hand. After writing the blog, I put the day away, focusing briefly on the following day's weather and road conditions before sleeping. Rarely did I look back to the day or days we'd already ridden. Rarely did I look ahead more than one day except to determine what might be headed our way because of upcoming storms or winds.

What is amazing about that experience is one day, October 3rd to be exact, I woke to realize we had just 20 miles left. There would be no logistics to consider before bed. There would be no campground or hotel stay. There would be no hanging the clothes out as soon as we parked so they would have time to dry. There would be no more oatmeal made with hot tap water for breakfast.

Somehow, each of those "but not todays" had added up to 3,102 miles that stretched from Astoria, Oregon to Washington, DC. But how?

I definitely rode all those miles. My daily blog posts with the date stamp prove it. So do the hundreds of photos, as do the memories of each town, each funny, scary, or difficult thing that happened along the way. And yet, somehow, I still can't make all those days, towns, and events add up to riding across the United States.

While in Bemidji, Minnesota, I had the opportunity to observe the headwaters of the Mississippi River. I have no recollection of ever seeing the Mississippi River before, though I may have as a small child. However, I've seen pictures and listened to the songs. Johnny Orton in the Battle of New Orleans sings, "In 1814 we took a little trip, Along with Colonel Jackson down the mighty Mississip."

The Mississippi is a grand river capable of handling boats and barges. It supports entire towns and industrics. Though not one of the Seven Wonders, it is certainly on the list of "must-sees" for many Americans and those visiting this country.

But do you know what the "Mighty Mississippi" looks like at the headwaters in Bemidji? It is not mighty in any way. It is nothing more than a babbling brook, easy to cross with bare feet and rolled-up pant legs. From that point onward, the Mississippi River moves forward each day, gathering speed and might until it becomes the Mighty Mississippi. Our trip was like that – starting out as a puddle and ending as a roaring river.

The dream-like quality of the experience and our inability to make our brains accept that we really did it is something Bruce and I have talked about quite a bit. We think we understand why we are having such a difficult time. It's about eating elephants.

Do you know how to eat an elephant? One bite at a time.

Do you know how to ride across the US on a tandem? One pedal stroke at a time.

How do you do anything in life that seems too big or too impossible? Take it one baby step at a time.

If I had focused on Washington, DC rather than the next hill, the goal would have seemed unachievable. In fact, the goal would have been paralyzing. Focusing on the next pedal stroke, however, was not difficult at all.

In actuality, I didn't ride across the United States. I rode 72 individual days, each day having individual qualities and circumstances. Although my blog listed each day as Day 1, Day 2, Day 3 until we got to Day 72, my mind was on "Today." When put together, all the todays added up to a grand adventure as large as the Mississippi River.

your turn...

Focus on now

Recall a time when you had a huge thing to accomplish, that you knew would take a good bit of time and effort. Did you find yourself fast-forwarding into the future?

How would the challenge have looked if you broke it down into bite-size, achievable pieces?

Does this change how you'll approach challenges moving forward?

Use the journaling space on the following pages to write down your thoughts.

_____

_____

_____

_____

_____

_____

_____

_____

_____

_____

_____

_____

_____

_____

RULE 6
Define Your Success

What is your definition of success? This is something to consider as you go on an adventure or tackle anything in your life. Imagine pedaling each day for 72 days, reaching the Marine Corps memorial, and still wondering if you've been successful in your endeavor. Talk about making yourself miserable!

Isn't making it to the end the true definition of success? Not necessarily so. Let me illustrate by using an example from long before I met Bruce and ever considered tandem cycling – the birth of my first child in 1989.

After my first OB-GYN appointment, I signed up for the birthing classes. My hubby and I did what we were asked to do. We wore loose-fitting clothes, we took off our shoes, we brought a small tennis ball for massages, and took copious notes. By the end of the eight weeks, I was ready. I knew how I was going to handle my labor – all natural. I had no need for medications if I just did the breathing.

Then life happened. My blood pressure started going up too high, and I began retaining immense amounts of fluid. A week before my due date, the doctor directed me to the hospital to be induced. Because of my medical issues, I was not allowed to walk around. I had to stay in bed, flat on my back, attached to a medicine drip and a blood pressure cuff. The nurse used something akin to a crochet hook to break my water, and my labor was started for me.

After ten hours of contractions that were consistently three minutes apart, I was exhausted but had only dilated two centimeters. Nothing was going as planned, so I chose to have an epidural. Although the medication sped the dilation along, my pushing was ineffective, making that stage last another three hours. When I finally delivered my nine pound, four ounce baby boy who was perfect in every way except for a cone-shaped head and splotchy skin, I was happy ... but not as ecstatic as I thought I should have been. Why?

I was busy berating myself for not doing it correctly. Yes, I had the baby here. That should have been considered a successful end to a difficult day. But I believed I didn't "do it right." I had to use medication and couldn't push him out without help from specialized equipment and medical staff. Clearly, I had failed at childbirth, I told myself at the time.

My son is now in his mid-30s. I have long since given up on the proper way to give birth. In fact, I told my three girls as well as my daughter-in-law that the correct way to birth a child is to get the baby here. Period. That is the true definition of success.

The reason I tell this story is that Bruce and I had to make some adjustments to what a successful adventure meant. We went into it with some unrealistic expectations. We wrapped ourselves in a bit of pride that could have derailed our triumphant completion.

Our intention was to cycle every single mile between Astoria and Washington DC. No matter what. Period. So for the first three days, despite huge climbs up, we stayed firmly on the bicycle, even when common sense dictated pushing would be a better option.

What would our friends and family think if we had to push the tandem? What would those reading the blog think? What would the motorists passing by in cars think? The answers were too onerous to consider.

At some point during the third day, Bruce stopped the bike on a hill. I assumed we were taking a butt break, but

I was wrong. Bruce declared, "This hill is too steep. We're going to push it up."

Bruce wore a heart monitor when we cycled to help him determine the amount of effort he was putting in. When going up these monstrous hills, his heart rate would hit the 150s and have little time to recover before starting the next climb. By the end of the day, he was exhausted. He could not do this day after day after day.

When he decided it was time to push the tandem, his heart rate was about 120, and we pushed up almost as fast as we rode. It made more sense to save his energy for the hills we could climb rather than waste it on the hills we shouldn't.

At first, I worried about the cars going by and what the drivers were thinking. I also gloated when we got to the top and got back on the bike, knowing the new motorists would have no idea we had to get off and push. Gradually though, I stopped caring what the drivers or those following the blog would think. Bruce and I were the ones out there day in and day out. *We* were the ones who knew our limitations. We were the ones who had to decide how best to journey from the coast of Oregon to Washington DC. When we eliminated pride, our trip grew easier, and our success was more assured.

We also had to rid ourselves of the expectations of others. This became apparent when I received a comment on one of my posts detailing a wonderful 84-mile ride fueled by a tailwind. This ride came after a week of 30-mile days, and we felt fortunate to be able to make up so much mileage in one shot.

One of our readers didn't see it the same way. Instead of acknowledging the tailwind as a perk, they asked, "Don't you feel like you are cheating?"

This particular reader's definition of a "successful" adventure was one in which all days were uphill into a headwind with horrible weather, bad roads, intense heat or rain, and crappy accommodations at the end of it all. Which is fine, if that reader had been having the same adventure that we were on. But, this "break" that we had was a delightful push that made our day better.

I admit I found myself irritated that someone thought that we were cheating ourselves out of a more grueling, and therefore somehow more authentic, adventure.

Here was my reply:

In a word, NO. And here is why. For every tailwind, we have a headwind. For every downhill, a hill goes up. For every cool and breezy day, a day is hot and stifling. For every "glamorous" campground, a campground is primitive. For every restaurant meal, there is dehydrated food. For every flush toilet, there is something far less friendly!

Yes, some days are easier than others, so we do what any smart cyclist would do - we take advantage of our good fortune - and I don't think it's cheating to do so. Anyone who would like to argue has to ride through Oregon and Washington on a fully loaded tandem first - then we'll talk!

Some folks seemed to believe that taking the Lewis and Clark route was somehow less "successful" than taking the Northern Tier, with its five mountain passes in the first six days of riding. For others, riding less than 70 miles a day or having to take a rest day were sure signs we were not finding "success." Still others believed unless we did everything on our own, we would not be successful.

We easily shed most of these ideas. However, learning to ask for and then receive assistance did take a bit of doing.

We chose to cycle unsupported, meaning we did not have a car following us to offer assistance or carry our gear. We also chose to be alone rather than ride in a group.

Despite riding unsupported, this did not mean we had to ride without help. Sometimes help was sorely needed. Other times, it was just handy. In all cases, we learned to welcome having it, whether it came from church members, other cyclists, or community members.

In one blog post, I wrote:

Isn't it wonderful to have community?

Bruce was spent. I was spent. We were both hungry. The winds were getting worse. My weather app showed they would soon be above fifteen miles per hour. The temperatures would also increase to well into the 90s.

So, we did what any smart cyclist would do. We got help. Bruce and I are not above asking for help when we need it. The purpose of our ride is to do something adventurous and to raise money for Toys for Tots. We aren't spry chickens anymore, and we don't need to prove anything to anyone. Do other cyclists press on? Sure. They deserve a pat on the back for their efforts. But I don't think that diminishes what we have accomplished.

So, today, we got Mr. Durosher, a resident of Dodson, to take us to Malta by pickup. We are now staying in the Sportsman Inn, have eaten at Dairy Queen, took a three-hour nap, and are eating pizza for dinner.

All in all, we skipped about 200 miles of cycling, which gave us the ability to continue our journey and make it to the end goal. We learned our limitations and realized there was no need to put ourselves in danger to prove anything to anyone.

Rides to avoid horrible road conditions, construction, and torrential rains and high winds were not the only help we received. We slept in people's homes and backyards. We were given food gifts like cookies and Pepsi. A wonderful lady paid for a two-night campground stay in Michigan. A nice man stopped to help us put the spare trailer tire on after a flat. And the list goes on and on.

The amazing thing about the assistance is how it arrived – quickly – every single time. We would realize we were in trouble and, within minutes, aid materialized. One of the most notable examples was the evening in Havre, Montana.

We were staying in an RV-centric campground that had a few areas available for tent camping. As we readied for bed, someone walked over to chat with Bruce about our journey. I was busy getting my gear together for the morning. Glancing at the time, I knew we had a long day ahead of us and wanted to go to sleep.

Before long, this man said, "So, which way are you headed? East or west?" When Bruce said we would be going east, the man said, "Do you know about the construction?"

It turns out that Route 2, the only real way through to our next planned stop, was torn up for ten miles. And by torn up, I mean the road was completely missing. Motorists were driving on the dirt roadbed with lead cars in front, while construction workers used water trucks to keep the dust down.

There was no way we could trail-ride on a tandem. What could we do? It was almost eight o'clock at night, and we were planning to be riding again in less than ten hours. We didn't know a soul.

Bruce got busy and made a call to a few local church leaders and then waited. We heard back from one who lived on the other side of the construction. Once he understood our plight, he said, "My wife can help. I'll send her that way tomorrow in the pickup truck. What time can you be at the beginning of the construction?"

Within minutes of finding out we had a huge problem, our problem was solved. The same happened when storms were coming toward us in Minnesota and again in Michigan. It happened again when we were too exhausted to ride, and once again when there were no campsites available and the next town was too far away. It even happened when we needed a part for the bike, but the local shop didn't have it in stock.

On riding day 72, as we rode through Roslyn, VA, I saw the American flag on an angled post. It was the flag on the Iwo Jima Memorial – our destination. Alternating between broad smiles and enormous tears, we pedaled the last half mile. We had succeeded, on our own terms and with the help and support of so many along the way.

your turn...

Define your success

When faced with something you want to achieve, do you tend to focus on *how* you'll succeed? Preparation is of course important ... but do you leave room for those inevitable glitches and surprises along the way?

Think back to something big you accomplished ... were you able to stick to the plan the entire time, or did things change and evolve in real time? How did you feel when things had to change, or you had to accept help?

What would your experience have felt like if you allowed space in the plans for the "hows" to change along the way?

How will this change how you define "success" on your next goal?

Write down your thoughts on the next few pages.

RULE 7

Set Aside Fear

I don't recall being anxious as a child or as a young adult. I don't believe I was anxious as a young mother either, although I'm sure there were times our pediatrician would beg to differ. But along the way, life often came at me in unpredictable ways that resulted in some hefty anxiety.

By the time Bruce and I decided to have this adventure, I had anxiety about a number of things – pretty much whatever I was fixated upon. For this journey, my fixation was Lolo Pass.

The majority of our training rides happened along the coast in North Carolina. If you've never been to the NC coast, I recommend it ... unless you're looking for hills. The coastal region is flat for miles before reaching the ocean's waves. Oh, you may find a small rolling hill here and there, but for the most part, the entire area is only slightly above sea level. To give you an idea, our home sits on one of the high spots at our end of the county, at a whopping 35 feet.

Although I was not an expert cyclist, I clearly understood we would find the hilly sections of our adventure the most difficult. Not only would we need more strength to pedal up the hills, but we would have little experience doing so together.

In addition to the physical experience and training, I soaked up information by reading blogs and journals of other cyclists who attempted a transcontinental journey.

Adventure Cycling Association (www.adventurecycling.org) is a nonprofit organization that promotes bicycle travel and touring, advocates for better cycling conditions, maps bicycle route systems, runs cycling tours, and publishes magazines, books, and a newsletter. Our original plan was to ride the Northern Tier, an Adventure Cycling route, from Anacortes, Washington to some point in Maine.

Numerous blogs included stories and details from people who had completed this route. One blog in particular made me grateful for Bruce's ability to be prepared for any situation. This father/daughter blog documented their trek through the series of five mountain passes – which has no towns and no place to buy provisions. They hadn't prepared ahead by packing everything they would need and ended up begging for food from campers along the way.

I soon realized I was fearing those first several days. The Northern Tier was difficult right from the beginning with one day of riding before hitting five high passes, each at more than 5,000 feet elevation, in a row. We were still a full year from our start date, and I was already dreading the first days of the ride.

So, I did what I always do. I researched a little more.

This time, I searched for tandem cyclists who went on the cross-country journey. I found fewer blogs on this topic, and of those I did find, not one followed the Northern Tier. In fact, most didn't start on the coast at all, bypassing the mountain ranges.

Although the mountain passes scared me, I didn't want to admit defeat before I started. Plus, I wanted Bruce to meet his goal of riding across the US, so I kept searching until I found a couple who not only rode a tandem but coincidentally rode the exact tandem we owned.

They chose to ride the Lewis and Clark Trail as their way of getting through the mountain ranges. They first crossed the Coastal Range in Oregon, and then the Cascades. By their posts, neither were horribly arduous.

The biggest climb was through Lolo Pass, which took them across the Rocky Mountains and into Montana. After lots of research and many iterations, we decided to follow this path – at least until we got to Missoula, the home of Adventure Cycling. From that point, we would make our way back to the Northern Tier.

I sighed with relief. One mountain pass about a month into our ride versus five mountain passes in six days seemed much more reasonable. Nonetheless, Lolo Pass became my nemesis and the fixation of my anxiety.

Every hill I climbed as we trained, I compared to Lolo Pass. Every difficulty we experienced, I compared to Lolo Pass. I even got it into my head that once we crossed Lolo Pass, the climbing would be over, and we'd have nothing but rolling terrain all the way to Washington, DC.

My fixation on Lolo Pass intensified as I read blog post after blog post about this place. I scoured the map of the area, doing my own calculations to determine the percentage grade of the incline. I calculated the mileage up, our typical speed, and the number of days it would take to reach the summit. From the moment we chose our route until we reached the top, I dreaded those days of climbing.

Bruce kept reassuring me it wasn't going to be as bad as I thought. We met and rode with a cyclist for a few days early in our trip who had been on that exact route.

He said we would do just fine, but I couldn't believe him. This was Lolo Pass – THE hill that beats all hills. If I could do Lolo, I could do anything. *I just wasn't sure I could do Lolo.*

Finally, we arrived at the Lochsa Wild River Scenic Highway, which culminated at Lolo Pass. Over the next 140 miles, we would be without phone service, Internet, motels, and restaurants. Much of what we would see while cycling hadn't changed since the time of Lewis and Clark, with the exception of the two-lane road through the park.

The next three days were spectacular. Yes, we went up for three days, but the grade was easy. We were able to keep an eight mile an hour pace for most of the ride. Every turn in the road brought a new vista, one that seemed to be the most beautiful I had ever seen – until it happened again and again ... and again. That would account for the more than 700 photos I took in three days of riding!

On the first night, we stayed in a primitive campground and connected with a lovely couple; they even took us out to dinner when we eventually rode through their hometown in Pennsylvania. On the second night, we camped on the side of the river and marveled at the clarity of the stars. On the third night, we made it to Lochsa Lodge, the only motel in the entire 140 mile stretch, where we enjoyed a great meal and the knowledge that in the morning, we only had seven miles to go to reach the summit.

It wasn't until the fourth day, when the climb became so arduous that Bruce pushed the tandem for five miles while I huffed and puffed behind him, did my initial concerns seem valid. Even so, by noon we were at the top; by four, we were eating ice cream at the Adventure Cycling headquarters; and by six, we were consuming pizza at the campground where we stayed for the night.

We had made it! All that angst had been for nothing.

What I didn't realize was, although Lolo Pass was demanding, we were not through with the steep inclines. In fact, the following day we navigated two extremely difficult hills that almost put Lolo Pass to shame – not in height, but in effort.

Quickly, I learned about a sign that would send shivers up my spine: **Chaining area ahead in 1/2 mile**. Wherever trucks need chains in the winter, it means the hill has a grade much higher than we can ride. On the day after Lolo Pass, we passed that sign twice – once on Avaro Hill and again before coming into St Ignatius. My blog says it best:

> *The grade was 7 or 8% – so we pushed uphill for an hour. The hill is known as Avaro Hill.*

The downhill was great. It went on for miles and miles. And then? Then we had another HUGE HUGE HUGE uphill that required pushing. This grade was even steeper. Trucks went up in low gear with flashing lights. Bruce and I went up several hundred feet at a time before having to stop and catch our breath.

This downhill led us into St. Ignatius – where we were lucky enough to stay with the Jensen family. We ate a wonderful meal of hot dogs and fresh corn.

Today was not as hard emotionally. I think it is because I didn't know what was coming!

As you tackle something big, you are going to find some parts of the journey are harder than others. I learned while riding that it's almost impossible to determine what parts will be the most difficult. What is hard for one person may not be hard for another; what's incredibly challenging one day might seem so much easier on another.

Because I was fixated on Lolo Pass, I wasted needless hours worrying for no reason.

Just as importantly, because of my fixation I neglected to fully prepare for the realities of the adventure beyond Lolo Pass. Yes, the big pass was complete, but this in no way meant no more hills. We had many more during our

ride across the United States and many days were far
harder than Lolo Pass had been.

I learned as we navigate life, we need to be as
prepared as we can be for what lies ahead. We also need
to be prepared to be surprised, both pleasantly and not
too pleasantly, by what we find around the next corner.

Adventures, life, change – none of these are fully
scripted. It's up to each of us to take the journey, knowing
we will be tested and believing we will pass the test – one
way or another.

your turn...

Set aside fear

Have you ever been truly anxious about something hard you had to do? Maybe it was a tough conversation with a loved one, or a difficult medical procedure. Maybe it was a physical challenge, like your first 5K, or an emotional challenge.

What were you afraid of about that situation?

Did the things you feared actually happen?

How might setting aside your fears help you face your next big adventure? Are there things you can do now to ease those fears and make them less scary?

Write your thoughts on the following pages. And if you feel ready, share your fears with someone you trust, so they can support you through this.

_____

_____

_____

_____

_____

_____

_____

_____

_____

_____

_____

_____

_____

_____

_____

_____

_____

_____

_____

_____

_____

_____

_____

_____

_____

_____

_____

_____

RULE 8
Know Your Why

Over the course of our 3,000 mile trip, I came to realize that every day's last two to three miles – whether the day had been long or short, hot or cold, up or down, headwind or tailwind – were hard. Every. Single. Day.

This might make sense if the final miles of a laborious, sweltering, uphill ride with a headwind are hard. If the entire day's ride was difficult, we are tired and struggling to finish by day's end.

It makes less sense when the day is short, and the conditions are favorable. Why should riding 20 miles of gently rolling hills on a beautiful sunny day with a slight tailwind come with a difficult ending? I learned it usually has to do with mindset.

When we come close to the end of our day's journey, I lose focus. I begin thinking about what I will do when the ride is over rather than on completing the job at hand. I allow myself to feel all the aches, pains, and discomforts. I recognize I am running low on energy. My mind is already at the end of the journey, even though I am still trying to pedal the last three miles.

I believe the same thing happens in life; enduring to the end often is not easy. How many times have you started the day with great intentions – and by midday, those intentions are slipping away as fast as the passing minutes? How many times have you started a project only to complete 80% before hitting a wall, all desire to finish gone?

This inability to endure to the end might explain why many relationships fail, people no longer enjoy their work, churches lose members, non-profits have difficulty retaining volunteers, and more. Unless we are 100% clear on our "why," we stop pedaling when the going gets tough.

I recognized this phenomenon early in the trip and wondered how I could overcome the grueling nature of those last miles. The first thing I tried was trickery. As we started out in the morning, I would add five miles to our projected mileage for the day. So, a thirty-five-mile day became forty. In that way, I figured by the time we got to the dreaded final three miles, I'd already be at camp.

As you can imagine, this did not work. Throughout the day, despite repeated attempts to state the exaggerated number of miles left, my brain was doing a bit of quick subtraction. When we got within the real two or three miles of our day's goal, I would bonk.

I also tried stopping and fueling a few miles before the bonk occurred. When we had five miles to go, I would ask for a break. During this break, I would eat a snack, drink plenty of water, and enjoy the scenery. Then, we would ride the last 30 minutes or so to our destination. For some reason, getting back on the bike was even harder than having stayed on it to begin with.

I tried to distract myself. During the last hour of pedaling, I would put on some great music to take my mind off the miles ahead. This did help at times. Although the miles were still difficult, the music made them a wee bit more tolerable.

The real answer, however, is not trickery or distraction. The real answer lies in having a clear understanding of why I'm doing this. What impact will completing this have on my life? What changes will I be able to make in my life knowing I have accomplished this?

When we keep our reason front and center, we can endure – and indeed thrive through – our challenges.

Take relationships, for example. The beginning of any relationship is fun and easy. We are learning about one another. We strive to please the other person. We always show up as our best selves. Whether this relationship is romantic in nature or not, this is known as the honeymoon phase. However, all honeymoons must come to an end, and when they do, the real work begins.

If your relationship only exists because you've tricked yourself into believing something that isn't true, or you are simply distracting yourself while you grit your teeth and go through the motions, the relationship is likely to end badly. At the very least, there will be little joy for you in that relationship.

On the other hand, if you are an active partner in the relationship, working to find and create joy, spending time moving forward together and accomplishing goals, the relationship will be far more fulfilling. The same is true for occupations, experiences at church, raising children, and even going on adventures.

In the end, I found the best way to handle the last two or three miles required two things. The first was acceptance. Yes, these miles present their own special challenge. Focusing on the task at hand is difficult when the end is so near. Yes, I am ready to stop. I learned to accept this truth without feeling any guilt about it.

The second requirement was gratitude. If I focused on something I was grateful for during those final miles, my attitude changed from one of misery to one of joy. Maybe I considered the view or a beautiful flower growing along the road. Maybe I noted a hawk circling overhead or a rabbit munching on some leaves. Maybe I acknowledged the favorable winds or the cooler temperatures. Maybe I found a silver lining, like finishing up the day in time to enjoy a dip in the lake. When I sought to find some good when my legs were screaming "nothing is good," I found those miles went by easier – most of the time.

What about the days when acceptance and gratitude were not enough? I leaned in to my why, pushed myself through it, and vowed to work on acceptance and gratitude even harder the next day.

your turn...

Know your why

Think back now to a time you made it through something difficult, something you had to take one day at a time.

Why were you doing it? Were you passionate about it? What did you hope to gain by achieving it?

Was there a day you wanted to quit?

What made you keep going?

Where did that beautiful endurance come from?

Write down your thoughts on the next few pages.

_____

_____

_____

_____

_____

_____

_____

_____

_____

_____

_____

_____

_____

_____

_____

_____

_____

_____

_____

_____

_____

_____

_____

_____

_____

_____

_____

_____

_____

_____

_____

_____

RULE 9
Never Quit on a Bad Day

Not long ago, I sat with my daughter reminiscing about her marriage when I realized that on her wedding day, I had not yet met Bruce. It seemed inconceivable that the man I rode across the country with had not yet entered my life. Had there ever been a time before I loved him? My daughter felt the same way. Was there a time before marriage? Before children? Before the life she was living?

Intellectually speaking, we are both aware that, of course, time existed before – before finding our soulmate, before having a family, before the adventure. Somehow, our minds dulled the edges of 'before' while focusing on the now.

Several days along our ride were grueling, making even rugged Marines throw their hands into the air and say, "I didn't sign up for this!" At the end of days like these, our thoughts would naturally turn to ending the adventure. What were the logistics of quitting? Would we rent a car at the nearest airport? Find a church member willing to drive us? Continue a few more days until the logistics made more sense? But we always went to sleep to "think on it" rather than act.

We chose to sleep on it thanks to a friend who reached out to me on an abysmal day. I could not imagine getting on the tandem one more time – or ever again. I could find nothing fun about this adventure. It felt like it was time to give up and go home. I'd said as much on my daily post.

Before heading to supper that night, I received a private message. It read:

"I understand the emotions and the need to cut it short. I would suggest never quitting on a bad day. You'll always regret it and wonder if you made the right decision. Consider staying a few nights in one spot. Once refreshed, you may decide to start moving again. You may not make it as far as you like in the end – but goals are for direction and reaching for – if they change along the way – that's life. You have accomplished so much, so whatever you do is the right decision. Just

remember you are awesome cyclists, awesome
individuals, and an awesome couple."

What sage advice. Never quit on a bad day became one of our mottos. We would consider quitting ... and then knew to wait. Inevitably, the winds would change, we'd have a good sleep, the weather would cooperate, we'd experience incredible scenery, or meet amazing people.

Just a few days after hearing from my friend, I wrote this post:

Although our ride was long today, it was great. About
halfway through, we were stopped for a quick
break on the side of the road. The sun was
shining. There were black-eyed Susans lining the
road as far as I could see. The wind was blowing
- from the correct direction. I said, 'I wish I could
feel just this way for the remainder of the trip.'

I was happy. Content. Strong. Encouraged. I wrote this down so I would remember this feeling on days that weren't so wonderful. I needed to remember this happened just a few short days after wanting to quit and go home. I now knew time has a way of changing everything, making me ready to conquer the world again.

Bruce and I also learned a bit about tandem time. Imagine, if you will, spending every day for just over three months no more than three feet from someone a majority of the day and night. Bruce and I, who had only been married 15 months and knew each other less than two and a half years, were only separated when using the bathroom.

We rode on the tandem together. We snacked together. We ate together. We slept in the same tiny tent together. Even when we were in a motel, we were crammed in with all our gear, with no room to spread out. We went everywhere and did everything – together.

Thanks to all this togetherness, we learned quite a bit about one another. It would have been so easy to use that knowledge to push buttons for the reactions. Except … we would have had to live with the consequences.

Riding a tandem is no more difficult than riding a single bike. You don't have to pedal harder. The rules of the road are the same. It isn't more difficult to balance. However, it does take teamwork.

For instance, here's the drill for getting started once we stop. First, Bruce throws his leg over the bike. Then he plants both feet on the ground and steadies the tandem. I wait until he says, "Okay, I'm ready." I rotate the pedals until the one on the left is at the bottom, put my foot into the strap, and say, "I'm going over." I wait to hear him acknowledge this fact, and then I swing my leg over and plant myself on the seat. Then, I raise my left pedal halfway to the top and say, "Ready."

Now, it is Bruce's turn. He gets his left foot into the strap and checks the traffic. Once he is ready, he says, "On three. One, two, three." We both push off with our right feet and turn the pedals a time or two until Bruce stops pedaling with the right pedal at the top. We both put our right feet into the straps. I tap him twice on the hip to let him know I am ready. And off we go.

The same is true when we dismount. I can't swing off the tandem until he has his feet firmly on the ground. If I do, everything will come crashing to the ground. Not following our practiced protocols leads to disastrous results.

Tandem riding also takes compromise. We met a couple while on the Greater Allegheny Passage (GAP) in Pennsylvania. They rode across the United States on a tandem and hated it. They are both expert cyclists on their own and riding the tandem meant they had to find a middle ground for their cadence. I had never considered this because, having not ridden in years, Bruce adopted my cadence as his own. I realized Bruce had adjusted his riding habits to account for my preferences. My preference is to turn the pedals slower and have more weight when I press down. I don't spin the full circle with my feet by both pushing down on the pedal and then lifting on the strap. I'm more of a 'stomp on the pedal' kind of rider, so all my forward thrust comes from pushing down. Bruce, on the other hand, gets continual thrust by spinning the full circle and prefers a faster spin and lighter pedal load. In the end, I learned to spin a bit faster and lighter than my preference, and Bruce learned to spin a bit slower and heavier than his.

All this teamwork and cooperation takes effort and is nearly impossible if the captain and stoker are not happy with one another. We learned this fact the hard way.

At some point early in the trip, I said something to Bruce that didn't sit well with him. I don't remember what I said. I also don't remember if I was being purposefully snippy or just situationally so. Nevertheless, Bruce was not happy with me. We rode about ten miles in anger.

Instead of a free flow of conversation, all my comments were met with terse one syllable answers. Plus, on most occasions, Bruce is a smooth captain, making me aware when something unusual is about to happen, telling me when we are going to shift, and being aware of my preference for a heavier pedal load. On this portion of the ride, none of those things happened. He didn't do anything dangerous, but he was not overly worried about the stoker on the back.

We arrived at a Dollar General where Bruce got a Pepsi, and we both got a snack. When it was time to get started, I said, "I'm not getting back on the bike." Bruce stared at me with wide eyes. "What?" So, I repeated myself. "I'm not going to ride the tandem until we work out whatever is going on."

The trip was hard enough without the tension. I figured I was in a great location with a restroom, food, water, even air-conditioning. I wasn't going to move until we fixed the issue.

Our first attempt failed before it began. Bruce gruffed, "Fine. What do you want to say?" I said, "I don't think you are ready to work it out. I'm going to eat my snack over there (pointing to a space on the sidewalk in the shade several yards from the tandem). When you are ready to really talk, let me know."

We sat that way for about 15 minutes. The next attempt was much better. Bruce was able to communicate his displeasure with my earlier comment. I was able to explain that I didn't mean it the way he took it, as well as apologize and promise to try avoiding similar statements in the future. He was able to apologize for how he handled his anger. We got back on the tandem, and though a bit tense at first, things soon settled down into our normal rhythm.

We also slept angry one night in a tent the size of a queen bed. It had been a long day, ending with several miles of construction that eventually dumped us into a busy downtown area. We were tired. The GPS wasn't giving us accurate directions to our campground. I grumbled. Bruce grumbled back. I re-grumbled and rather than let it go or work it out, I held it close and kept it until the next morning.

We set up camp, only communicating when absolutely necessary. We ate dinner without speaking. Bruce went straight to bed after we ate because we rolled up to the campsite so late. I wrote my blog, then crawled onto my side of the mattress, making myself as small as possible so as not to touch him. Two hours later, when I was still not asleep and feeling the cold, I pushed my back against him for warmth but in a way that let him know I was still angry. It was a miserable night, which made the next day miserable because my sleep was fitful.

Because of our circumstances, disagreements were both inevitable and inexpedient. We had to figure out how to communicate our displeasure quickly and in a way that fostered understanding and healing. If not, we'd spend a miserable day riding or a miserable night pretending to sleep.

During this adventure, Bruce and I determined we packed about 20 years of marriage into three months. We learned a lot about one another, and we learned to appreciate one another's strengths and differences. We learned how to express ourselves without being contentious, to determine what things to let roll off our backs, and to confront things when they needed confronting.

As of this writing, Bruce and I have been married for five and a half years in earth time. In tandem time, that would be about 25 years.

All of this is to say Einstein was right: The rate at which time passes depends on your frame of reference. I've known Bruce forever, and it has only been a short while since we met. The worst day in the world is never going to end, and it's a distant memory supplanted by sunny skies and a row of black-eyed Susans.

Time has a way of changing everything, so never quit on a bad day.

your turn...

Never quit on a bad day

As challenging as this trip was, I wasn't going it alone ... even if it felt that way at times.

What are you currently going through? Are you alone in it, or is there anyone else involved who has a stake in your success?

How does this change the way you feel about enduring the challenge?

Are there ways you can compromise and communicate with the people riding along with you to make it easier to stick it out? What's one thing you can do right now to improve the ride?

Write down your thoughts on the next few pages.

_____

_____

_____

_____

_____

_____

_____

_____

_____

_____

_____

_____

_____

_____

_____

_____

RULE 10
Continue to Dream

When we decided to traverse across the nation on a tandem bicycle together, I was 55-years-old, and Bruce was 67. It took another two years to make the dream a reality.

In no way were we the poster children for this adventure. I was a cycling novice, overweight, anxious, with limited camping experience. Bruce, though much more experienced, was nearing 70 and deemed 100% disabled by the Veterans Administration. Riding all day and sleeping on the ground at night was going to take considerable effort.

My reasons for wanting to have an adventure had nothing to do with cycling and everything to do with my desire to prove something about myself to myself and to those I loved.

After 14 years of emotional abuse in my previous marriage, I no longer believed in myself. I doubted my ability to do anything, including such mundane tasks as choosing the right peanut butter, a choice which had the power to paralyze me. I wanted to show the world that I still had worth and value. I needed to attempt something so far outside my comfort zone that others would assume there was no way I could accomplish it. That way, when I succeeded, the proof would speak for itself.

Bruce's reasons, on the other hand, had everything to do with cycling. Back in 1976, Bruce read an article in Sports Illustrated detailing the first group of cyclists known to ride across the United States. According to Bruce, "A group of unprepared college students were conned into riding from California to Virginia during the Bicentennial. They had no helmets. They wore cutoff jeans and rode on old, heavy bikes with horrible gearing. Despite their lack of planning and gear, every one of them made it. I wanted to do it with them, but my commander wouldn't give me three months off – go figure. I've wanted to complete a transcontinental ride ever since."

Can you imagine waiting 44 years to make a dream come true? That is exactly what we did.

I'm confident what we did looked nothing like what Bruce would have done had he ridden when he was 30 or 40 or even 50. We took longer, rode shorter days, spent more nights in motels, and had more rest days than he would have allowed himself prior to retirement. Because I wanted to accompany him, he chose to ride a tandem rather than ride a lightly loaded single bike. Because he was no longer a young man, our load included such luxuries as an air mattress and a real pillow. But he didn't let the minor changes needed to accommodate his age and my level of ability keep him from achieving his dream.

Prior to meeting Bruce, I had already determined I was too old and too tired to do the things I wanted to do. I was too old and tired to write a novel. I was too old and tired to learn to play bridge. I was too old and tired to learn to play the piano. I was too old and tired to take up ballroom dancing. I was too old and tired to ... what? Live?

Then I met a man who not only was older than me by a dozen years, but one who seemed not to realize it. And one who pushed me to be all I could be regardless of my age, my circumstances, my mindset, or the limitations of my body.

As we went across the United States, I often wondered what he was thinking. How did it feel to accomplish something that had been a dream for a better part of his life? He said little about it, but on two occasions, he did share his feelings with me.

The first time was as we entered the Lochsa River drainage that led to Lolo Pass. We rounded a bend in the road and saw the most picturesque scene – it was beyond anything I could have imagined, despite seeing photos of similar settings. It was truly breathtaking.

After stopping to take a photo, Bruce said, "I've waited 44 years for this." Then, despite the fact he will protest and say I'm telling a fib, tears flowed down his cheeks.

The other time happened as we stopped in Roslyn, a mile from our destination. This time, he had no words at all. Just tears and a hug, letting me know I had been instrumental, in spite of my fears and abilities or lack thereof, in helping him fulfill his dream.

I will never ride across the United States again. Not because I can't but because I have no desire to do so. Bruce, on the other hand, would love to do it again. He also has a desire to ride from the Keys to the top of Maine. I'm excited for him to consider these new goals for himself, just as he encourages me to consider my own adventures. Unfortunately, his brain cancer diagnosis may keep him from ever riding again.

I was blessed to find Bruce when I did. His willingness to include me on his grand adventure healed parts of me that were broken. He has given me the space to fly, fail, and grow in a way that hasn't been part of my life in a long time. He has helped me believe I can continue to grow and succeed and have grand adventures as long as I choose to do so.

There is something about going on an adventure that is addictive. No sooner had we come to the end of our Double-Butted Adventure than we were trying to decide what to do next. We chose to ride the Coast of Maine, completing a 320-mile ride from Kittery to Bar Harbor in September 2021.

Dreaming is a choice. Bruce could have said at age 69 he was too old to attempt such a ride. IIe could have said a person with his disability rating is too disabled to attempt such a ride. I could have said a person with my lack of experience was too inexperienced to take such a ride. I could have said a person with my weight was too fat to take such a ride. We could have let age or ability or any number of issues, including a global pandemic, keep us from achieving our dreams.

Or we could realize these issues certainly play a part in how we will handle the details, but they do not have to keep us from our destination. And that is exactly what we did.

your turn...

Continue to dream

What do you dream of accomplishing? It can be any "size" dream; it doesn't have to be an epic months-long journey. What do you truly wish you could do?

Are there reasons why you think you can't achieve your dreams? Do those reasons make you give up before you even start?

What if you change your mindset around those reasons, so you could see them as challenges that can be overcome while you figure out how you'll move forward?

Does that change how you view your current dream? Does it make you want to dream even bigger?

On the following pages, write down your thoughts and see what new ideas come out.

Teri M Brown

EPILOGUE

As we arrived in Arlington, I had an epiphany. I could do anything I set my mind to. It wasn't a matter of "can I do it?" but a matter of "what do I want to achieve?" What happened next, I realized, was up to me.

My husband tells everyone that the person who started the trip with him was not the same person at the end. The person at the beginning was afraid and unsure of herself. She believed she had little value. She knew she was a failure at life.

However, one mile at a time, one pedal stroke at a time, that person transformed. The adventure gave me time to reflect, obstacles to prove my mettle, and joy in every accomplishment. The adventure helped me heal and then grow beyond the woman who cried over peanut butter. I barely recognize her now ... although I think of her with more kindness and respect.

Although I no longer have a need to prove myself, I love rising to a new challenge. I haven't limited my adventure seeking to physical pursuits. I am now working on my fourth novel and my first children's book. I've started a podcast, and I want to learn how to paint with watercolors.

More importantly, I'm working to hold the lessons I've shared with you close to my heart, using them each day to increase my joy and satisfaction. My hope is one of these little lessons touched you, encouraging you to become – happier, healthier, sillier, braver, more serendipitous – whatever it is you most desire.

I've shared my rules with you. You are welcome to use them in your life ... and I also encourage you to think deeply about your dreams and desires and write your own rules for making them come true.

What will make you happier, sillier, braver, more serendipitous?

What dreams will you allow yourself to dream?

What adventures will you commit to, in spite of all the reasons not to?

What are your rules for your next big adventure?

your turn, your rules...

_____

_____

_____

_____

_____

_____

_____

_____

_____

_____

_____

_____

_____

_____

_____

_____

_____

_____

_____

_____

_____

_____

_____

_____

_____

_____

_____

_____

_____

_____

_____

_____

_____

_____

_____

_____

_____

_____

_____

_____

_____

_____

_____

_____

_____

_____

_____

_____

_____

_____

_____

_____

_____

_____

_____

_____

_____

_____

_____

_____

_____

End Notes

Saxe, John Godfrey. (1873). *The Blind Men and the Elephant.* J Osgood.

Niebuhr, Reinhold. (1932). *The Serenity Prayer.* Union Theological Seminary.

Driftwood, Jimmy. (1936). *The Battle of New Orleans.* (Driftwood's poem was made into a song in 1959, published by Bradley Studios.)

Adventure Cycling Association. www.adventurecycling.org. Accessed October 21, 2024.

Acknowledgments

I would have never been able to write these words had it not been for my husband. He encouraged me to take an adventure that changed my life and continues to encourage me to fly as high and as far as I can dream.

I'm also grateful to my mother who, unlike many others, understood the need to go even with the pandemic in full swing. Her advice? "Don't wait. You never know what the future holds." If we had waited, we would have lost the opportunity when my husband was diagnosed with cancer.

Finally, I want to thank my four children, my three bonus children, and their families for all their support and encouragement before, during, and after our ride.

If you feel so compelled, I highly recommend Toys for Tots as a Foundation deserving of donations.

If you want more details about our Double-Butted Adventure, I kept a detailed blog of the journey at: https://www.terimbrown.com/team_dba.html.

About the Author

Born in Athens, Greece as an Air Force brat, Teri M. Brown now calls the North Carolina coast home. In 2020, she and her husband, Bruce, rode a tandem bicycle across the United States from Astoria, Oregon to Washington DC, successfully raising money for Toys for Tots.

Teri's debut novel, *Sunflowers Beneath the Snow*, is a historical fiction set in Ukraine. Her second, *An Enemy Like Me*, is set in WWII, and her third, *Daughters of Green Mountain Gap*, is a generational story about Appalachian healers. Her short story, "The Youngest Lighthouse Keeper," came out in the anthology *Feisty Deeds: Historical Fictions of Daring Women*.

Her latest work, *10 Little Rules for a Double-Butted Adventure*, is an inspirational look at the life lessons she learned riding across the United States on a tandem bicycle. Learn more at www.terimbrown.com.